An Elusive State:
entering al-Chwm

CW00607315

STEVE GRIFFITHS

Cinnamon Press
Independent Innovative International

Published by Cinnamon Press
Meirion House,
Glan yr afon,
Tanygrisiau,
Blaenau Ffestiniog,
Gwynedd,
LL41 3SU
www.cinnamonpress.com

The right of Stephen Griffiths to be identified as author of this work has been asserted by him in accordance with the Copyright, Designs and Patent Act, 1988. Copyright © 2008 Stephen Griffiths.
ISBN: 978-1-905614-60-8

British Library Cataloguing in Publication Data. A CIP record for this book can be obtained from the British Library.

Designed and typeset in Palatino by Cinnamon Press.
Cover design by Mike Fortune-Wood from original artwork by Carlos Torres based on a photograph by Marilyn Pietroni.
© Carlos Torres, used with kind permission.

The publisher acknowledges the financial support of the Welsh Books Council.

Printed by Biddles Ltd, Kings Lynn, Norfolk

Acknowledgements

Parts of this work have appeared in *Poetry Wales* and *Planet*, and have been broadcast on *The Verb, BBC Radio 4*.

Thanks to Weidenfeld and Nicolson, a division of the Orion Publishing Group, for kind permission to quote from Claude Levi-Strauss, *The Savage Mind*. The epigraph from Edward Said's *Reflections on Exile and Other Essays*, p.582 is used by kind permission of Granta Books; the epigraph from *Invisible Cities* by Italo Calvino, published by Secker and Warburg, is reprinted by permission of The Random House Group Ltd. The epigraph from Joseph Conrad is taken from *Nostromo*.

Note on Pronunciation:
al-Chwm: 'ch' is pronounced as in 'loch' for Scots, or 'Bach' for musicians; 'w' in Chwm is a short 'oo'; 'm' as in 'mother'.

Contents

The very idea of identity involves fantasy,
manipulation, invention, construction.

Edward Said

Perhaps all that is left of the world is a
wasteland covered with rubbish heaps,
and the hanging garden of the Great Khan's
palace.   It is our eyelids that separate them
but we cannot know which is inside and
which outside.

Italo Calvino, Invisible Cities

To be hopeful in an artistic sense it is not
necessary to think that the world is good.
It is enough to believe that there is no
impossibility of it being made so.

Joseph Conrad

To the ones who kept me going:

Gareth Aicken, Sean Baker, Wendy Bolton,
Val Bynner, John Hywel, Robert Minhinnick,
Rob Storey, Carlos Torres

An Elusive State:
entering al-Chwm

al-Chwm

amlwch: n. abundance; also, a small town on the north-east of Ynys Môn

1

The place I grew up is called abundance.
My not knowing Welsh
was not knowing this,
flowering in adulthood
one side of a fissure.
Circumstance and time
are two thieves shaking with laughter
but in other spheres I trudge
toward responsibility
for truths and lies in language,
sitting on the verge
at times with my bags.
This is written in the wind:
why not here?

2

Half a century of cataracts
over round stones that were eyes
to heaven, of water chuckling
minutely through stained brickwork
and I emerge into al-Chwm
with a sudden jolt of trust
with the relief you feel when you explode
out of a tunnel in the Underground
to a crash of leaves and speed and light,
the roar's end.   Then a quiet animal
homecoming.

3

al-Chwm is an inversion
of fulfilment and language,
mindful of children
growing up displaced
with their years not rightly focused,
and those for whom
the simple is at first too obvious,
who can only ride a bike
with a partner looping up and down
on the other pedal, on a steep hill
with a bend at the bottom,
and there's traffic.

It comes from an inability
to look abundance straight in the eye.

4

al-Chwm's a town on a concealed point
that comes to you when you're ready,
when the mist lifts, stripped of its poison,

a town that strains at the leash
that slips out of my hand.

The Book of al-Chwm

Entering al-Chwm

It began and ended with the barking of tethered dogs,
a hundred street lights for the non-existent carouser,
nobody up who was up to any good
but nobody was up,
footfalls exaggeratedly soft in the house,
the fridge appearing to boil defiantly
in its limelight,
ordinary things reversed
in a town like any other
that had never slept, nor ever would.

A man carries the place he comes from
on his back as he unravels,
it is transformed with every step as he is.
Others in his peripheral vision
shift their shape, but it is always he
who is running through a defence
with a mazy run that slows
and the game ratchets up to a blur
of speed and wonder, the tackles come
in a series of thuds within him
and he is on his own,
the commentator faded to their mutual relief,
and the judgement:
he was meant to pass the ball but didn't.

He is reconstructed as he diminishes
by schoolmates he hardly remembers
who have carried him forty years without noticing,
✓ by the milk of human interference,
and he carries their vowels for them
that jostle for his attention in gatherings.

Friends wrote a different essay
when they were eleven
and collide a second time
in the same time and place,
their electrons and neutrons
arranged for a different party.

He drifts, not noticing
the decisive moments under his feet.
The town he turns in to is al-Chwm
with his pancake stack of faces
that consolidate to the one book
with its pages of flour and disappointment,
dried milk and prevailing smile
collapsed into each other,
with his waiter's tree of dishes
for the approval of the town he's made
that will come out to meet him.
Many meals, many traces, but the dogs
bark for each other, not for him.

This is al-Chwm, they say:
it is permitted to drop unnecessary loads.
There are memories he will declare
nothing to declare, green channel
and there will be nothing we can do.
It appears that what happens is allowed.
He finds the people of al-Chwm
wear mirrors on their clothes,
their currency is uncertainty,
their traditions rich
but indistinct.

Their monuments leave much
to an imagination shaped
carelessly by weather and time,
preserved for a minute that lasts.

Their songs resonate in the memory
as in a dome—it's acoustic
rather than detail they celebrate
though there are fragments
strangers recognise,
and those they bring—
it's not clear which.

Those who seek refuge here are safe:
the code for acceptance is a capacity
to raise one eyebrow
and they have joined you, or you them.
Thus a concern for justice is unknown
which brings much relief,
and al-Chwm is immaterial to the Fall
which fell past it, unobserved.
The parallel has replaced the afterlife.

The al-Hambra rescued

In al-Chwm, the world's wonders
are given a break to recover
from all the prying and footprints and exhaust:
they lie disregarded in the fields.

The al-Hambra is abandoned and forgotten,
shifted stone autograph by autograph
to the site of a chemical works
on a promontory, where lichen and moss
were an aspiration in a boom of foghorns.

The subtle Arab gardens
move up and down again
on pulleys set beneath the waters
in forgotten ways, hanging
and fragrant, facing cold peaks.
They are still about heat, but its memory,
and the memory of an inquisitorial
staring-mad rigidity,
a suppressed unhappy childhood.
They are replenished
with subtle rain and desertion.

Ideas on the use of the air

In al-Chwm at a moment of creation
a fighter was venting its tantrum
over the low green hills as they do,
breaking the hearts and minds of the livestock.
It was a compact swallow driven
by, with, from an apocalypse,
and it froze.
It remains suspended
over the town, largely forgotten
and there is nothing to decompose
the pilot but a thin sun.

The townspeople develop a myth
of seizing back the pilot's innocence.
Unlike Jesus, you can see him
up there, whitening.
Like Him, make of him what you will:
he showers alone,
away from the other boys.

I don't know whether this is relevant,
but over London where there is always more
beneath a smaller sky,
the heavens are stacked
with planes ferrying souls
with sun-cream and dark glasses
and warm jumpers for cold nights
till they become a continuous,
ascending hum.
They fade in the memory
as a form of storage over London
where the dead go, circling,
unable to leave the pull of the light.

A moment's autocracy

There is no divine authority
among the people of al-Chwm;
but they have heard the song
and know they will never enter
the changing labyrinth
of the lark's throat.
Inviolate authority's invested
in a moment of that throat,
its gracenotes thrown loosely
but as they fall they are adamantine
then lighter than air again,
a riot of butterflies
moving across a valley.

Language movement in al-Chwm

It has been easier to describe
the approach than the being there
so far. As people penetrated
the outskirts, what they usually said
was brittle and encrusted,
their articulation sluggish.
As they came towards the square
then it was that they encountered
clouds of their syllables
boiling up as clouds do
and turned outward
so you saw that they had linings,
then the air was keener,
most of the words the same
at first sight
yet their composition different.

Moral reactions
took a physical form,
animate and mute.
To patronise, for example
meant the end of hope
which curved back upon itself,
a planed shaving
that revealed old wood.

This led in time
to an absolutist tendency
in al-Chwm
who were for a vegetative state.
Their custom was to partake only
in the silent interplay of elements,
the many sounds of skin
against surfaces,
against absence.

The meaning of terminal

Is it a terminal condition?
Is it a retirement home?
Is it a utopia?
Why should I answer my own question?

No.

Its dynamic quality, cunning
is common as dirt here
in the cracks of its stones
and between toes,
it's built on watchful stillness
amid the intricate
dance of its insect life at dusk,
the learning of thousands of sudden
changes and close calls in flight
and then abandon, negotiating these,
it's all in the deep wrinkles of those
who stay a winter season.
Between high and low cunning
the al-Chwmian aims pretty good,
from practice
clever in circumventing.

For the young the days
are a circular growth,
a relay that lengthens like tree-rings
in the widening trunk
as the years shorten.
When you come round again
there's always someone
or something waiting for you
and you grow in the comfortable
oppression of villages, watered
with unnoticed ambiguity
until you need no faith.

Below the surface, a stillness
related to what's below tundra.
Therefore al-Chwm's fertility
is slow, and its seasons.

Some way off it is driven past
by a man from behind the walls
of company and sound
with a concealed memory
of miles around him.

Later, al-Chwm will be heard
in a cricket whirring feebly
two valleys away:
it can minimise itself like a screen.

Then it may rise to a shout
but he will not be there then:
al-Chwm will have passed him by.
His mother said no when he asked why.

The property of dreams

While I was dreaming in al-Chwm
I bought a house.
I tried to master
the reverse siesta,
waking briefly
to rehearse my dreams,
find my house,
put it in order.
Now we drive toward our destiny.
For a hundred miles of motorway
a spider clings to the wing-mirror.
A family wait in the house:
for them it has served its purpose.
You want to supplant the lives
out of them, and you realise
why purchase of room
is a capital offence in al-Chwm
which means your spirit dies.
Beware the fulfilment of dreams.
As you reach the doorstep,
in an act of heroic and loyal
self-harm, the space vacated
by the vendor may collapse.
Stand with your back to them
and your dreams will emerge
as neighbours, as stubborn
and brave spiders.

Steal away

There's a room of transition
at the slightly shabby end
of a branch line
closed years ago,
where you are visited
by an embarrassment
of sins of the heart.

They are persistent,
those old adolescent
crimes of meanness,
the seeing another's individuality
or hunger as a shadow
that became a lead ingot
in your ageing pocket.

Still they bring you
the small presents
that diminish you,
they know no other way
but the way
of the mirror
of the act.

There's sometimes
no need of forgiveness,
as when you pay the bill
discreetly in a restaurant
and turn away,
that is, if ever
you have the wherewithal.

Through surfaces

You find yourself
dipping through surfaces to al-Chwm,
skimming
across a flat calm
under still, grim skies
\ of stratus with a hint of gentleness.

Your craft is a flat stone
small enough and round
to fit in the crook of a finger,
and you think hard with your eyes
shut, because everything about you
is contained, of St. Bridget
who made the crossing
on a piece of Irish turf
to al-Chwm, and continued
on her miraculous course.

Having gasped for breath
all your life under wave
upon plausible wave
of unnecessary explanation,
you are cured of the need
to know who the skimmer is.
You don't want to know who did it,
the butler in the scullery or the fairies,
with a bloodaxe, a rubber glove
or a serpent in a tree
or an ingenious combination
of all three:

there's no tall explanatory boat
to carry you away,
just a hard little body clutched
and spun, the sound
of the spray, the speed
and meticulous angle
of a hard surface
that doesn't quite penetrate,
over and over beyond
what you calculated possible
and you dip below,
sink with the finely
varied oscillation
of a feather,
discover
another kind
of play of weight and lightness
or miraculous discourse.

Light and perspective

For a few feet beyond the window
of a dining room, a patch of garden
is illuminated
or a brick wall
flickers, seething, half-tamed,
what's beyond it unimaginable
where barbarians
or suburbans live their lives
among species we could not acknowledge
in our sleep, unable to grasp
the range of possible organs,
appendages, displays
and functions.   What is clear
is that they lack parts
we consider necessary.

There at the end wall
a lamp is wreathed
in a turbulent shade
of red leaves, like a house
with blinds crashing
at open windows, a small
settlement viewed from outside
where you breathed it deeply in,
or you tried.

In al-Chwm since the lights
of a house are inward,
darkness licks the walls,
the accepted stranger.

From her home in a trench
in a city, surrounded
by sirens, debris,
irregularity,
a brave architect dreams of a town
designed retrospectively:
it begins with weathering and settlement,
a population in decline.
As she watches
the leaves change colour
and strange dogs materialise.

Back to back

It's a terrain that's increasingly mountainous.

They love the word troglodyte.
The caves in their mind face south.
From shadow that never warms,
those of the north
face visionary wastes
then for a short sharp season
a fertile counterpart.

Gifts of darkness spill daily
toward those of the south
from the shadow side
of the hills, and they shrink
to the warm stone
at the back of the caves.
In the end it gets to you.

Those of the north say
it is better to work from obscurity.

al-Chwm's lacunae

1

An attractive village,
a well-worn shoe:
its scuffs are memories
or nurtured cares.
Books are not burned
but brochures are
because they spill the beans
till there is nothing left

but a vulnerable secret.

2

People are hungry
for a guiding intelligence,
they seek it everywhere,
but the collapse of the penal code
in al-Chwm has a simple
organic ingenuity:
the universal sentence
is appointment to the police.
The criminal's the object
of the warmest vigilance
as through the streets
he drags the weight of aspiration
to accountability.
The offender cherished most
forgets a secret
all around remember
and in this way gossip
evolves into principle of trust:
each has a story unique
but unknown to him,
kept by his circle
and buried with him:
all share a high responsibility;
all an unknown confession.

3

The bigger the state
the duller the senses,
the smaller the pigpens,
the blander the mushrooms,
the more desperate the crocodile
conversing on the hill,
the lonelier the need
for the penetration of space.

4

Nevertheless in one history
al-Chwm expands
to the size of Siberia
because half the people of the world
want asylum there
from the other half:
in this way it shadows
America, pumped up
distractedly beyond sense.
As a warning to al-Chwm
the weapon of the world's aspiration
is turned on America,
to which it has no answer.

5

The two paradigms of power
that gave the individual
the blessing of an intimate regard
were Stalin's
and the great American penetrations.
al-Chwm follows a policy
of standing up against a wall
hoping that no-one will shoot
or ask it to dance,
then that a long decline
will prove attractive
for which the reward in al-Chwm
is to be left alone.
It encounters
the conundrum of Venice
that required full exploitation
for its degeneracy to flower.

At this point the account
breaks off,
reappearing pages later
to describe a village
of the same name.
As always,
the durable answer
is fragmentary and brief.

Just enough

The once unemployed hang about in the square,
so many, to be taken in lorries
to the Elysian fields where they will work
three hours, enough to feel good
as promised once in the white heat
of technology: the hands hard,
the blood coursing, a vigorous
Sunday joint on the table,
vegetables you have dug
and no weariness:
the promise of the millennium.
Al-Chwm's up
for some kind of prize
but the judges get lost,
it's too small
like a best kept station
with no line but a platform garden
and there are so many silent tracks.

Powers

There were intruders,
though all maintained
there were no borders.

There was a man with a wild bark
who made a woman tremble,
who was after an inheritance:
for hours they could not ease her.

He should not have been alive
for an oesophagal peseta
gave his words a penetrative ring: groats
and dinars plugged his anus and his eyes.

They cultivated a protective
savagery, they experimented
with the directed curse,
and to their astonishment

his lips and his fingers ballooned.
It was too successful:
they were jubilant.
They discovered guilt

that came like floating seeds
in the autumn.   They worried
that the melting of the Poles
would mean it came no more.

Kinship

al-Chwm searched for the Arab kinship
visible from the name
and could find none at all,
so little it seemed as fishy
as the disappearance
of the magnetic pole
over the next hill,
and the next.

Only later they discovered
DNA in common
with a small Saharan people:
great humidity out of the arid,
the underlying kinship of opposites,
like solidarity
only dancing in spirals.

They shared a meal of their different gutturals,
their tonalities
and their different teas
and afterwards they walked in a vaulting space.

Families

A sticky issue that led
to the disorder
before the disorder of al-Chwm
was the disposable family:
they littered the countryside
like blown plastic on bushes.

Siblings took to it easily
with their prodigious chests
built for seeing off.
There was a moment of balance
when it was hard to tell
which was the parent
then you could make them out
as they shrank, grasping
at their children like limpets
till the young were mature enough
to express impatience
and the begetters slipped away
one by one, resigned
as if fingers had to let them go
or more brutally, pecked off the rock
at last into deep water.

Unique stories of lineage
were lost, and a common origin
reinforced
of man's first disobedience,
not necessarily
all bad.

In al-Chwm, as the pig
in every garden is unique
to those that know him
there was no one model
or building block of the state,
there was wherever you found love
looking for berries
in a wild grove
telling yourself
you had husbanded them to maturity
when what was unique
was the discovery,
and sometimes how late,
a fully rounded individual
off the peg.

Then children knowing more,
reminding you you know things
or not:
the wide screens at the back
of their throats flare
like a drive-in movie
with only the stars around,
they command
masticated scraps
of experience.
Thus the outside seeps in
through the future,
pervious and supple as movement
through time should be,
to permit generosity.

Cant take any more

16 v 22

41

Forgetting

Through the years the fame of al-Chwm
spread like slow gum
on a forest floor
and hardened,
causing injury to the fauna
that did not adapt.
Each dawn it was reinterpreted.
That way the place was not followed
and found freedom.

Things began not to work,
there was a rash of compensating
mechanism, which failed
as well.   Spiritual growth
occurred in inverse ratio
to convenience.   The demand
of competence stepped on heels
no more.

An undiscovered fold
in the cortex of the brain
came to prominence,
a faculty of stubborn parody
of half-remembered science
generating flightless
craft that made sense
like the dodo
only when thrown,
and enigmatic sandwich toasters
that could simply not have been true.

In time, capillaries
starved with long bewilderment
thinned and withdrew.
The fold was left open
to the wind in the brain.
It turned generous as wool
on a memory of barbed wire,
grew reverent before stories
and began again.

Moments

Houses in al-Chwm
have a book of oneness and moments.
It is all right to wait,
for the book to be
composed for a while
of blank pages.

Families read from it
after dinner, often
gazing in silence
at the empty page
like a sheet of cloud,
the young no less nostalgic
than the old
who are no less full
with a fierce longing.

These are not books
of the hurried notes
of industrious people.
There is a moment
when the wind is at rest
and nothing moves in the undergrowth,
and still nothing is committed to paper.
Nor should the wine be turned to vinegar
through long fear of the exposed line.

Moments that led to wrongness
are particularly valued
and catalogued.
Though furtive,
such moments allow their faces
to crease into a smile
when they are recognised.

To know when to choose them
is to transcend,
not time,
but one time,
one time at a time.

al-Chwm chosen

Their hearts sank.
There was this intersectional chink
of time and justice
in a perverse cosmos—

for a twisted universe is possible
without a personal god
with a history,
like a twist of lemon
to embitter it—

where they found
they were expected
to judge the others.

Britain was its own misshapen asteroid
spinning clumsily
with an atmosphere
as you would say
she entered the room
and there was an atmosphere,
and this patronised village
with its untracked record
was obliged to judge the others,
man, woman and child
(as the meek shall inherit,
and don't ask
what happened after).

It refused:
nothing happened,
there was the silence
of angels passing
till the cog slipped
on to another winner
whose subjects
might not be so fortunate.

Myth of origin

Banished
from the garden of hell
for self-consciousness.

He knew
that behind the garden
was another:

in it there's time for you
and space, and their ingenuity
he colluded in,

peering out from behind
a wall of old ivy, safe
in a shelter half way up a cliff.

Amnesia

The technological amnesia
of al-Chwm
gathered pace.
An optometrist
with a penchant for nostalgia
was known as the optimist,
and was fully booked
for months ahead.

Corkscrews

They learned to disassemble
their molecular structure
like a Loony Tunes cartoon:
screwing themselves up
into corkscrews
they would go,
kerpow!
through vegetable matter at first
then brick
then hard rock.
Their first experiments
were painful,
but through long years
to understanding the liquidity
the bones need
to swim about the body
as in an aquarium
of fluid outward form,
they added the physics
of karate and Merlin
with a fixed ambition
that served them in the end:
they would fling themselves
and land on the grass
in some unimagined continent,
panting with uncontrollable laughter,
dying like swans,
crushing a cowslip bell
where they lay,
exhibiting, I'm afraid,
little curiosity
and much cliché
but astonishing the inhabitants
with this difference
from the destroyers of the New World:

their golden vice
was the point of singularity
where all the laws break down
and nothing outward is changed.
Like swallows
they always knew the way home
to al-Chwm.

Game

They learned
from the nervous Scandinavian deer
they herded
about fucking on the hoof
then being off again
almost without breaking stride,
uncoupled,
unhinged.
It evolved into a game
of rushing and patience
that combined
mental and physical power
and letting go,
and letting go
that made for a strenuous landscape,
its prospects
erotically charged.
The indoor version
was a great success, played
from room to room
of great public buildings
made for the purpose:
they used it to cleanse
their parliament at recess,
to restore the supple joints
of their politics.
For spectators
it shared the shortcoming
of motor sport:
as the protagonists flashed by
to another room
you had to imagine
from the sound.

In their decadence
both the game of sex
and the parliament
were competitive,
grew fractious
and burdened by too many rules.
Short cuts were devised
through the chambers of arousal
to the rutting room.
Some old timers complained
of a loss of discipline,
others remembered
joyous abandon,
and how absence makes the heart.

The untroubled

A therapist
while combing through her basement
like a mermaid
found a mirror
born in the lightless
desert of a vacuum
that would force its welcome
on any hapless passing matter.

She said, the paper tigress,
that to discover
a connection between two phenomena
was to realise
its absence up to that moment
as loss.

In this version, the history
of each event
to its emergence
was a long rewinding scream
of grief and hunger
joining others
back to an unbearable beginning.

There are limits to the reality
we will sustain:
we backslide to plead
with something else
to take responsibility,
the bank to take on the debt,
accepting the illusion of interest
rather than declare it null.

In al-Chwm, the untroubled
saw nothing as nothing,
and that even applied
to the latent generosity
seen by the optimist.
Why not nothing?
Have the spiritual discipline,
the respect
to let things ease into themselves
as into a pair of trousers,

to leave off.
Things begin to happen.

Not for transport

They invented a cart of fine steel
that would take off,
manoeuvrable as a boat
with a pole, light
as a dandelion clock
where they could stand
at the bar of the sky
and drink and point
and tell stories
and piss on the clouds
when they felt the need:
sometimes
spectral urine
like a line of verse
would unfold
out of the sky.

The science
was a frivolous pursuit,
the manufacture
(against their nature)
not the point,
a remembered limb.
They built
from the ground up,
the wheels first,
those used by the Olmec
of old Mexico for toys
but not for the transport
of power and wealth
which were dragged
with brutality
along perfect roads.
They knew the answer had to lie
in a lightness of intention
in themselves and their loads.

Unfortunate commodities

One of the finer figures of a man
is made like a brick shithouse
the better for combat
for good living space
and fertile land;
another with a grasping reach
the better to get at the delicate
precarious berries
or to gouge the adversary.
They are made at least partly
to instil fear, and together
they are more than their sum,
but not by so much.
If they are small they thrive
because they are nimble
or alert, or can see far
or can advise or command
with force of mind,
or are gifted in hiding
or their sperm have a particular drive.

Now, when the clay tablets
have electrodes attached
and evolution's not a rising plane
but a horizontal line
to a state of wave and cable,
self-referential
and eventually dipping,
an interesting fraction
of these qualities
are in demand.

Much of a species
gone beyond its point,
we adapt with a customary
brilliance:
the road to the coronary
is a king-size burger away
for the humiliated primate
zapping its remote
in the faint, imprinted
memory of failure
from way back when the low status baboon
just got on with it
and died of loss.

Men have nothing to lose
but their anger
and there it is,
spilled over the road,
petrol,
do what you will with it,
America.

On this, al-Chwm tries
to take a position
outside of its humanity,
arms folded,
cornered and truculent,
the choice seething with maggots
that will cure wounds
and will have you:
either go back to the animal,
the whole accident
of collaboration
with an ecology
millennia
beyond reach now;

or else, slack-jawed before the box,
there's the suckled victim
in the free, humiliating cardboard hat,
yearning back to the coloured planet
he believes he came from
though he's been cut loose from that.

Then behind the rows of pudding-faces,
always
the unacknowledged face-puller,
the furtive glimmer
of awareness
with its sporadic flare-up
that threatens others
with a knowing provocative look
it can't hide, try as it will.

That is what endures
biding its time
face to the furrow
as long as it can,
blocking out the cries,
its heart a rare
subversive jewel.

Nightmare

There was a dark period,
a perverse marriage
of mind and sense
when leaders were chosen by smell
for their intellectual power:
a brimstone odour
of concentration
that putrefied
and decomposed
to superstition.
That which is not the progress of sceptics
interspersed
with long moments
of balance
slips back toward nightmare.

Who is to tell the difference
between stagnation and balance?
There is always a stupefaction unit
in fine uniforms
who watch for the momentary wise,
to stun them like flies
and who wish them a horrible death,
drowned in their own lucidity.
These are the revenant souls
of a sniffer dog drug squad
known for their devotion to crime,
to their nightsticks
and to living with certainty.

Outcome

Strategies of self-belittlement
came after the fear of empire
in themselves, something akin
to the growth of a sense of sin
but wrier, without abasement,
rich in experience with three times
the amount of garlic and coriander
they had first imagined, and the danger
not transcendent, but that they would lose
the time they had in their own eyes,
and the loss was in their own eyes.

The way of the metaphor they followed
was about giving things up
and gaining
in a cumulative striptease
where they would realise
how much they loved each garment
and the unique enclosure of skin
revealed beneath it
and each patch of sky above it,
as they stood there
in a gathering nakedness.

Alarm clock

It's time for death is it
when things get repetitive
and you know this is so
or you don't
and the pains crowd out
even the memory of pleasure,
when the children are just veiled noise
losing specificity
slowing down to a still
Dutch silvery interior.

Not while you recognise
that smell of dough rising early
from your own bread.
Not while you still believe you are interesting
though you may have become insufferable.
Not while you can distinguish
solitude and can populate it
with an increasing society
of voices out of their time
or with one grown sparse
in a green and charged exterior
behind glass
and some blackness moving behind
which is also you
and a golden sea before you.

Al-Chwm has nothing to offer
but acceptance
of the sweeping on
you know about:

death is the same everywhere
your smiling companion
that shifts through
and sifts through
every moment of your life,
licking your lips
till you feel nothing.

Beyond anxiety

Hidden in their preoccupation,
the work they did before the moment
they did not yet inhabit,
the staff at the hospital
grew distant.
The day was made
of successive ramparts
that a very small memory
played behind.
Patients colluded,
their look became glassy
above a retreated core.

One cure they found
was touching and grooming
though they needed too
the skill of solitude.
The nurse would lie down
with the patient
and look at the ceiling
as the warm stain of shared identity
spread through their haunches
as the lion with the lamb
and it was unclear
where one ended
and the other began,
as the cat spread out asleep
on the place of anxiety.

The need to suspend an epidemic
of decisiveness and acceleration
was met with an outbreak
of waves of panic in reverse,
the spontaneous freezing of crowds:

visiting strangers
would wander through them a while
and suspect a theatrical happening
or the commemoration
of an armistice,
till they caught on
with a yawn of relief.

The satanic writ of al-Chwm
was a yellowed paper
from one of those golden dawns
on the use of social systems
to suppress anxiety,
defeated later
according to fragments
for the clumsy optimism it was
by an empire that overcame its victims
with a wall of irresistible images
and slavering want that reduced them
to a fatally uncritical mass
and turned them against themselves:
resistance was killjoy
to the seduced
and was exposed to the full panoply
of a military complex.

This was a fable
the people of al-Chwm
could hardly believe
but strove to evade
with vigilant exercises
in derision, followed
by a periodic raggle-taggle caravan
in pursuit of the constellation
of their hopes.

After weeks of hard travel
(and to die on the journey
signified arrival, threads
to pulsating stars)
they would arrive at a rock face
where the arrangement of ropes
obeyed a change in gravity
and the climbers were pulled
toward each other
in an unexpected configuration.

Always,
if they travelled far enough
they would encounter strangeness
at a face of rock
and would take nothing away with them,
satisfied.

Entire hospitals
would up sticks
and do this.

Growth

1

To freshen and ruffle the air
the world needs
to be turned upside down a little.

For the length of a day
they would think very hard of themselves
as antipodeans, as an antidote

and the earth would be perceived
by evening
to be slightly out of kilter

they as undersiders,
renewed.

2

Their off-centredness
was reflected in hearth-gods:
pride of place was held

by the god of the wry
with smile-wrinkles
about the eye

who had a divine affection
for a notion of perfectibility
that encompassed flaws.

By him was a smaller figure
suspected once
to have been a garden gnome,

wearing, as a tribute
to the domestic foible,
clothes the man of the house

had shrunk in the washing machine;
and often he stood
in a burned pan,

a little warm thing
between partners.

3

In this realm beyond forgiveness
a wax arm for an arm, suspended
there below the mantelpiece

and a wax eye for an eye
were understood, when they might
have been a curse, chilling

in their dark place,
to be hung
like spectral hams

by well-wishers for the afflicted,
for curing.

Givers

There are moments
when the quality of the roar
in every history changes,
as the throttle opens or shuts.

The primitive dynamic
is the availability of food,
and a feature of the watershed
is warehousing:
the full stomach
then the song.

In al-Chwm
they measured time
from a moment
that brought sensuality
to the smell of boiling and salt
that pervaded the kitchen,
to the island surrounded by fish
that swam undisturbed
in the hitherto slow tempo
dance of devouring.

They celebrated the originator,
the shadowy bringer
of herbs and spices
who came in the form
of a nurturing hermaphrodite
with generous accoutrements.

After the meal the reflection,
then the song and the hunger again
with its memory of seasoning.

They expressed fulfilment
through metaphors of food,
the cycle of nourishment and excrement
and cultivation, to be cut off
by the bringer of grief
who would control the surplus
and so the ferocity of the myth,
who was haunted by dark aromatic
embers of Rioja
in vast chambers of loss.

The story warmed
and stirred their minds
in the end
with fearful and sentimental
befuddlement.

Transplants

A fugitive group
appeared in the neighbouring hills.
They had come together
by looking into each other's hearts.
They saw the earth differently,
dug roots with devotion,
snuffling when they were sure
nobody was about,
rolling in patches
among soaring trees:
leaves, mud and stalks
stuck to them.
They had been given
the hearts of pigs.
They looked into each other's eyes
and slipped away quietly.

Variations on the ear

1
Music

Taking it as read
that a species by its very nature
will be endangered,
they realised
from observing others
that without their personal music
they would die.

In the totalitarian folly
that is wisdom
undone by rage
gangs roamed from house to house
destroying the speakers
that spilled music
from across the world
across the room,

and just in time
before it was reduced
to a syrup of uniformity,
a desert of earwax.
They listened as the sea
roared and sighed
for months.

An audience too
they liquidated
not as you think,
but in time and in circles
that heaved in the form of waves,
the least musical learned
to tap out a unity
that was always in the air
on household instruments,
spoons, milk-churns
and catgut for which the cat
was venerated when alive.

From under the earth
with a sound
of a burrowing of moles
came strains
of ancestral music
that summoned the skill
and the work and the pleasure
that begins before you can walk,
lost voices and the plucking
of strings that meander
away from keys and back
into affirmation
you think is terminal,
that bubble up from the grave
with a distant sound
of subterranean picks,
of a liquid that pulsates
on through the body
till it reverberates
like a bell in the cranium.

To turn the soil of music,
enforced isolation
and a moment of savagery
were permitted, it seems.
Innocence grew again
like trees dressed
with candles and sequins
on still nights.

Hearing music on a breath of wind
they would die to be inside it,
driving it with their hips
and the sounding board of the palate
to affirm a greatness
in the small sound of the animal,
in the near-silence of ants
digging, the near-sound
of the blood in their own ears
and the deafening song of the fly
with whom they shared
a deviation of chromosomes
and therefore stories
exchanged over a piece of meat
half-burned on the fire
and left on the sand,
and they listened to the bass
throaty drone of limbs
that vibrate in darkness,
finally the fly's almost silent
dance of bodily unguents,
of the dawn of anticipation.

Then there was the pepper
that ran from a clandestine radio
hidden under some flight of stairs
under the stars,
crackling into life.

2
Restlessness in music

Al-Chwm had restless wells of talent
that emitted swarms of things
the population didn't want to think about:

so a background of chatter
and clanky music
soothed the internal voice,
moderated the performance,
shaved the concentration.

It's an industrious nation
that lives off sustainable argument,
the manufacture
of tranquiliser and enervator,
stimulator and distracter.
Under a brilliant onslaught
of the weaponry of the banal
conceived in a heartless library
soundless but for the humming lights,
the suppressed
stream of consciousness
became another bunk-level
of the unconscious.

People would go crazy
without their implants of music:
left to its own devices
the irregular rhythm of nature
struck them as a moral terror
run amuck, with its disorder
and its punctuations
of elitist silence.

Thus a new variation was added
to the historical parade
of cultures on a long, fugged
bender through a tunnel
of staple substances,
from strong ale with a little cheese and bread
(if you were lucky)
to coca leaves.

And yet, since both
fashion and natural selection
reach out through a sequence
of mistakes for the variable,
the adulterated, the perverse
(one a little faster than the other,
both in the form of a flattening spiral
where you expect to see
the misfortune of others
and which there were hairdos to celebrate)
there grew an irresistible fixation
for the artifice of silence
above the humdrum.

In a paroxysm
of self-induced panic,
in the altered state
of hunger denied,
for the good of the nation
in a precipitous revaluation
after a run on the mind
sonic wallpaper was banned.

Governments collapsed
in an anxious, shallow-breathing parody
of the origin of species:

under the first cabinet of a new regime
they played funereal music
with subdued flourishes
on the radio, then as the radicals
gained confidence,
the only permitted broadcast
was a gnomic poetry
with little reference to anything
anyone knew,
an island of five minutes' speech
in twenty-four hours
of tuning to a hiss
you could turn up
and scour for variety.
The population fell
on the minuscule ration of words
and devoured them,
regurgitated and chewed them again
like shoe-leather
till they were satisfied.

The storyteller who seized on
the twisting, evanescent phrases like flies
with a predatory quickness
and recalled the words
with the tongue of a striking lizard
was king
of the quiet wastes.

Shutters were opened on faculties.
There were motorways of silence
everywhere
that led them to memories
of the savannah
when they dropped out of the trees,
rightly made
to be vigilant and afraid,

picking up the stories in the grass,
distinguishing the sounds of danger
from the soft garrulity of the wind.

Circuits were on the mend.
There was a wall of mountains
behind the city
that could not be seen before
which some thought
was the placing of its humanity.

Deadly or not in al-Chwm

Anger was a rare incursion
but ire, that prophetic fury
was another matter
in the weather of the place,
upending tired thought
and blowing down boundaries.

Envy was brought by in-laws
from elsewhere, and withered
before a disinterested poise
located in the pelvis
and the nape of the neck,
that showed in the walk.
Some said that when the walk went,
the seed of envy
started to germinate again.
Old age strove to retain
the walk in the mind.

Sloth had its season
in youth and age
but was valued in the prime of life
and was a branch
of the study of time.

Lust, why not, peaked
like an erection
in a history lesson, distractingly,
then followed its declining curve
sometimes bucked
by joyful exception.

Gluttony was dependent on supply,
but formed part of the science
of intemperance
which suggested a remedy,
a ruptured circuit made good.

Pride found its own level
mocked beyond a certain span
or understood, through the mechanism
of a safety valve,
to be self-mockery
whether it was or not.

Avarice
was a simile
for unfulfilment,
its original meaning lost.

It was said that in early times
these things were subject
to a septennial audit
by an authority
which had slipped away
like the state at that time,
or the time in that state,
whichever.

Oscillation

Their poets were astronomers
and statisticians in their search
for significance:
they found a wobble
and spent lifetimes
describing it,
speculating on its origin
in a wonder
of scepticism,
sometimes arriving
at the partial explanation
before the next.

The astonishment of sceptics
is delicious
and not undermining.

Bending over backwards

Their humour became so deadpan
that faces of gloom
denoted hilarity,
and the smile
false stratagem
and an ingratiating style.
Thus they joined the cultures
of the backward flip
where a shake of the head
means yes
and a curl of the lip
is a come-on,
where at worst
the speaker needs
the help of mirrors
or consultants
to be sure of his own
refracted meaning.

Textbook history

1

Since they mislaid
the climate that made them
what they had been
centuries before,
they were few, and depended
on the known individuality
of the other.
Such was their cohesion
they forgot their place
and their identity
was in their wandering.

In time again they settled
and from a perceived
homogeneity
there grew an assertive flame
of purity, its origin
diverse as you like,
a new configuration
small,
concentrated
then churning outward
like a cloud of lies.

2

Your whole past flashes by

Outnumbered cigars
played poker for the desert
and the flooded land.
Their cards had no faces
or aces.

The oceans were thinking collectively.
Their triumph fulfilled a dream
of the common man
of the ruthless and inevitable
over the ruthless.
Collateral damage was again
the lot of innocence.

This time,
the demonstration of theory
was more thoroughgoing:
farmers woke afloat in a storm
in a mute laboratory,
victims, they believed,
of some malign intelligence
which turned out to be theirs.

Seafoam flying
on a hurricane
reclaimed an old imagined freedom,
unbought, unsold,
to be savage—

to behave in a manner
unrestrained by the stays
of civil norm;
of culture unfamiliar
to the established powers;

to be ungoverned;
to be fair game,
to restrain trade
since you fail to imagine goods
when they have no narrative
you have contributed.

Angels in the detail

1
Their screen

At an undetermined point
between the age of forty-five
and fifty-nine or so,
the population of al-Chwm
would realise they wore
the features of a dying animal.

Of all the tyrannies
that they had undone on their way
to make their periodic call
on equilibrium,
the hardest
was the tyranny of beauty.

They taught their eyes
to run like fingers, searching out
the muscles tugging
each according to its history
at the corner of the mouth,
the former tautness
in the face that sagged
between pitted lineaments of bone,
searching out the sequences
of narrative
in rumpled linen bedsheets
and the provenance
of roundness in the dunes,
the fullness of right places,
the façade neglected,

probing any feature
worn beyond distinction
by the wind and rain
with a kindly, curious
persistence.

Faces could not be ironed with impunity
at this point in their evolution
or descent: roots would spread
across them like an oaken choir screen
till one day only tendrils
could be seen
and nothing of the many-parted
voices or the stained light
behind them.
There was a boundary to cross
before the sum became the parts again,
worming independently
like many-parted voices.

2

Vigilance

Sitting by the body,
family and friends
heard mostly interference
to the sublime.
From just a few minutes before
they recalled
an impassive, slow demeanour
where a nuance
would occasionally flutter
like the flash of distant lightning
or the inkling of a dragonfly
or something bigger
quick in dense undergrowth.

Had they the strength
to receive the intermittent signal
from among the opportunities
seized up,
behind the eyes
and down some ill-lit corridors
they might have come upon
the party that had been there
from the start,
and somewhere at the centre
half-obscured among the raised arms
swaying as one from side to side
in adoration
lay some kind of royal box
or ark that cradled the berserk,
the irregular leap of the blood
at the core of the music
and at the heart of that,
a queen or singer
with fragmenting bones of crystal,
almost but not quite
immobile, with a small smile
responsible for orchestration.

It was this smile that surfaced now
at the corner of the mouth,
bearing the mark of the wheels
of wild times
that had driven over those features
with abandon
once, or not quite.

So many shallows, depths
and fantasies to plumb.

3

Long life

At an undetermined point
between the age of forty-five
and eighty-five or so, they knew
they would begin
to fail to recognise
the plumage of the new, its electricity
concealed in growing cowls
of darkness:
they'd realise they bore
the features of a dying animal.

Diminished
to a fear of waking
to dispense advice
with misplaced confidence
and with an inward tremor
visible to all,
they'd come round with a start

knowing it all remained to do again,
and knowing this time round
when it would hurt,
and whom, and worse —
o, they thought,
to feel no longer
the pull of earth's bright feathers,
o to reach out for the dimmer
in the already dark

4
Attention

The residents of al-Chwm
marked the fall
of sparrows, relatives
and those who worked the roads
with sharp attention
to the grace they bore away with them.

Their guarded optimism turned
on a conviction
that the common stock of grace,
light-clawed or -footed,
would be undiminished,
confident their children
by the age of ten
would each have gathered in
the name and value
(knowledge fused with function)
of at least four hundred species,
many of them minuscule.

It was in this their riches lay,
whatever the cruel disorder
of their own decay.
They were not replenished
through a shopping channel
but by the trembling
in every sinew of an animal
about to spring
on an oblivious detail;
an entire focus,
sweeping past the negative
capacity for the banal,
that gave them radiance
through every sense.

*I found myself in a place
where supposedly primitive
informants distinguished
about a dozen kinds of
snakes, sixty-odd types of
fish, more than a dozen
types of fresh and salt water
crustaceans, a similar
number of types of
arachnids and myriapods.
The thousands of insect
forms are grouped into a
hundred and eight named
categories, including
thirteen for ants and
termites. Salt water
molluscs of more than sixty
classes are recognised, while
terrestrial and fresh water
types number more than
twenty-five. Also at least
forty-five types of edible
ground-mushrooms and
ear-fungi. Even a child
can frequently identify the
kind of tree from which a
tiny wood fragment has
come, and furthermore, the
sex of that tree, by
observing the appearance of
its wood and its bark, its
smell, its hardness.*

The watershed festival at al-Chwm

The nature of time
was the eye of their storm.
They celebrated the momentous day
of the discovery
that time was not linear
and had ceased to be thenceforth,
when they set aside
the discredited question

    answered by death

    or by the flat wages
    of merely banished want
    with its storeyed carpark
    of arrival,
    the finality of its wad
    of never completed floors,

    or by the monotony
    of a final justice,
    sister to that of the chosen faith,
    each as corrupt as the other
    with their need for the damned,
    the gilt and kitsch of the leader
    and the led, the same bloody harp
    forever, the torturer's mantra.

Ah, progress,
shot down by the curvature
of the spine of time,
when what they realised they meant
was a starting point
decent enough to return to
after a day in the fields.

And every year the ceremony
of the slipping in and out
and then the breaking
of the keys to an imagined road
to an imagined capital,
the shedding of the absolute
with a queen of uncertainty
masked for one night
with a rubber face
who confirms them,
or does she,
as laughing and skilful
lovers of time.

The first symbol of the night
to be worn is the painted eye
at the back of the head,
so there can be no denial.

The second is the bicycle
denoting the curve
in the track of time,
how they follow it
like a rear wheel
as the road is made
and they are part
of its ingenuity.
Turned around
and placed on the nose
it's a pair of spectacles
and the spokes make the eyes
multifaceted.
They would carry elaborate
representations
of the vehicles of seeing
to a central point,
and the burning spokes
would turn them to trance.

Through the eyes of insects
in the heart of the night, renewal
does not need the stamp of humanity.
The revellers know
they are consumed in their turn
by the small, the numerous
and finely tuned;
and as the harbingers of day
creep indistinctly
with the dew of their cleaning machines
over the debris of broken masks,
a cup on its side, an empty bottle
and an abandoned wing,
it is they who know
with the first rays of the sun
that just to see it all with better definition
would be something.

Certainty

1

You cannot account
for the movement
of all the bacteria
in every shadow
forever:
there is always one
where arrogance will bide its time.

There was this critical loss
in the quality of attention:
vigilance became an effort
when the pinch of irony
slipped from the fingers.
Once the smile stopped
playing on the lips
there remained
an absolute
to pass on to the young,
just one flat stone
without which the sea
would be drained.
al-Chwm was gliding
into the dock
of the state of error,
in a downpour
fast and furious
of unintended consequence.
Thought to be decayed
from lack of use,
the organ of surveillance
took on its own life
and those of others.

This is a tale of control,
integrity and pestilence
regained.

2

al-Chwm was the place on earth
where life-skills were supposed
to run deepest
where fools were thin on the ground
but not literally,
where the detection
of bullshit and self-interest
was at its most refined;
where cures lay
at your feet
like diamonds
to be chosen,
or infections
to be farmed.

3

al-Chwmians discovered
in the eyes of others
that the way they lived
was the object of desire.
At first they were uncertain
whether this was flattery
or distorted by mirrors,
but disproportionate power
made its bed with vanity
and lay in it with clouded vision:
there was a flight of steps,
whether leading up or down
no-one could tell.
This policy was embarked on:

they needed children
with dark-rimmed eyes
and ill-fitting trainers
to bring out the best in theirs
who showed signs of indifference
and etiolation, it was thought
through a decline
in the incidence
of clutching hands from below.

To sharpen the edges of fear
for the bright ones to work with
they imported little bony refugees
with a business sense beyond their years
who had seen their relatives gunned down.

This was the attraction
of the client state.
On the horizon they could see
the dust of its coming.

With the new children
came parents in traumatised postures,
the domestic and industrial
cleaners of the world,
bred to be peasant farmers
but as ever both more knowing
and more innocent
than those they cleaned for,
sustained by a hope
that it was still the right valley
they were trudging across,
one they knew would grow deeper
between two mammary green hills,
tumuli that spoke before
of crops as much as death
and would again;

and through the investment
of a dying generation
they were sure
their children
would ascend the other side,
look down from beside a pool
and choose to remember
or forget.

4

Predictably, there were tensions
and a border hardened
like a scab that had grown powdery
and flaked away when left alone.
Blood from faces
that had pressed against the window
ran underneath it:
centuries ahead
walkers made a path
from the composition
of its soil.

The building of frontiers
stimulated the economy
with all the things that feed
prickly exteriors
and the fear of subversion
that sustains them:
there was opportunity
for border guards
and designers and cutters
of uniforms, manufacturers
of nightsticks, infra-red
cameras and sewing machines,

creating more demand
for the flexibility
of migrants, more
of the debilitating frisson of threat
and the ancient desire for police.

5

There were those who still held
to the old belief
that perfection of the life
was to be found
on the threshold of decay:
the skill was to prolong
the moment of neglect,
both divine and economic.

The difficulty was
that the tension on the frontiers
came from within
now they had discovered sin,
and there was no escape
from the running of horses
across a flat landscape.

The view that increasingly
prevailed in a climate of fear
was that what mattered
was an excluding skin of identity
whose emblem was the core
of an apple with its safe
snow-cavity, its off-white hall
with dark, curved,
self-referential furniture
that swirled to a still point.

What defined them
was a place of ritual
so precious beneath the surface
that it went unexamined.

The motto carved beneath
the throne, unseen
once their inside
was locked in:
any sacred nonsense to fight for.

All around, with the force
of a theorem, as the fear
of resentment grew
so did resentment itself,
thought to be mitigated
in the client states
by the value of currency
from those who had left,
but reinforced in truth,
every banknote
given a twisted face.

6

How does the positive shift
come, the collective sigh
that says a decisive 'enough'
as ever more darkness
approaches, piling
on tense mouths
experts thought
regressively
less generously set?

To put forth green shoots
from within an outwardly
functioning regime
that demeans the majority
is an inexplicable gift.

There's a moment
of critical force
in the ground
that provokes an avalanche
or an earthquake
or the tyranny
caused by one educated person
too many
who opened his mouth
at the wrong time:
this one came
from the collision of tolerance
with deep-vein self-interest.
It was the final grain
that dropped on an accumulation
of weariness, the floater
in every process
that puts progress in reverse
or full ahead,
that discovers the energy in the rest.
It was composed
of having it up to here
with being told that to be generous
was to be weak.

7

The hope now
was to rediscover
the al-Chwmians'
legendary gift for analysis,
for spotting smooth transitions,
sand in the machine
and remote light:
rather than strengthen the border
as the early migrants,
who would have slammed it shut
behind them, demanded,
the belief grew in removal
of the need in the client states
to uproot.

Descriptions began
to come in
from beyond the edge of the map
on tracks that led back to the heart
as to a peeling kitchen door,
paths that were variations
on an original complicity,
beside them
the occasional abandoned culture,
the invisible counterpart
of rusted tanks in the fields
and the unvalued faces
that lay behind them.

From these traces
they began to acknowledge:

the loss that came with accumulation

the scorn in themselves
for themselves
they had sown in others

the slow things they had put to the margin

the redundant body parts
found later to be essential

the plants despised
and found to be medicinal

the memory in the fingers
that with forgotten skill
made a trembling bridge of yarn
to a people
not yet deciphered —
then the divine restraint
not to intrude

outside the ramparts
of their own achievement
that had made them passive and defensive,
the capacity
to listen with generosity

that there is no way back:
there is only attitude

they were in love again
but this was a second marriage
with uncertain contours,
small unrecovered settlements
and the unguarded expressions
that inhabit them:
they would spend a portion of each day
searching the lines in others' faces
watching for the clouded eyes
of foreigners to clear.

Bookends

1

With the sucking sound
of a boot lifted from a bog
to leave its last print
inexplicably in mid-path,
the end was in the provisional:
strange events were dredged,
primitive fish out of the mud
that lose their colour in the light
and need to be frozen or consumed.
They make an unready photograph,
unwillingly presentable,
older than they thought they were,
fish that consider themselves
eternally caught in the moment.
The only false note
will be on the plate,
next to the ketchup,
not how they would wish
to be remembered.

2

Here are the ironed features
of the end, mounds planed
by the hooves and rain
of centuries;
the stones of al-Chwm
lifted bodily away
to build centres of power
with ever cleaner lines,
taking with them unbeknown
their stubborn blemishes.
There is this desolation
of reeds wheeled upon
by the wind,
bristling and swept
in a complexity
never repeated,
that stretches away
to where sky and distant hills
part company,
the earth's curve
creating an illusion
of open possibility.

There have been layers
of obliteration, the removal
of defining features
such as the nose of the place,
its capacity for insight
and delusion,
collective and individual.
There were people who knew
how to live here
and nowhere else.
It's what made them
vulnerable and envied:

caught in the headlights
of the invader
they would stare back
with an amused tolerance,
frozen forever
in the illusion of arrival
after a good meal
surrounded by friends.

They got their wish
to become elusive again.

This was an unfinished copy
of heaven, with half its qualities:
you will never be done
working out which half.
Things fade off uncompleted
like the tail lights of a thief
disturbed at his work.

Steve Griffiths was born in Trearddur Bay, Anglesey, in 1949. He has published four collections of poetry since 1980, the last being *Selected Poems* (Seren, 1993). In the Nineties he took a long break from writing and publishing, before an intense period from 1999–2004 when he wrote *An Elusive State: entering al–Chwm.*